"From Venus's world,
her words are gravitation,
self-gratification,
gentrification,
invigorating displacement,
displayed glorification,
kind of sounds like her right,
then again maybe on forward as she left,
love is everywhere,
but I do not love you directly,
no I will never love honestly,
she is confusing giving inspiration,
of positive nurturing of all she can...
with each and every hue-man possible,
to include all other levels of obstacles,
sub-particles too still we grow-up out as
hair molecules...

quite perspective rotating a different aspect,
rowing sayings reflecting mirrors off me waters,
touching wavy feelings people thoughts are always absent,
though this antenna keep grasping them artistically crafting,
you cannot mask your raid among masses of shiny rays,
you will be a dismayed fave avenue of anew trade,
who spoke reel into time,
rhyme designs rose wild I'm blind,
fore being foreward beyond ignorance and lies,
exactly where did my truth come from?
A little further past shallow martyrs,

filling me cravings with notes, pitches and glitches,
for every blink let void receive my riches,
an abyss physical mine cannot escape,
cape on my shoulders tucked proudly,
and have no weaknesses we can relate,
ship your tastes of wetness,
who sweetens dry bitterness,
being barren on top of surface,
I bear witness below flowing miraculous,
vineyards of dates rumbling out of control,
upcoming me geyser shook sprouting splashes splat,
squirting all me got giving pureness onto you...
and what you do with it?
You bottle me up sealed like no other kind,

eventually hatred will find me deep into
your cove,
you have to be guardian of your entrance
extremes carefully,
words from Venus's force explained may I
suggest as advice,
time is love fool never shake the dice."

5 LETTERS

Venus,

I never understood why me and you can never stand still. Why you busy in everybody else business? You can never leave earth alone. I be doing circles getting heated with intelligence to aspire our journey away from all the forces but you always wanting me to message letters. You never give me the time of day or night only on a specific timing...maybe we are too powerful to be. The galaxy might explode and cause galactic consequences if we do stop to just dance once. This is why I have long nights of coolness waiting on the opportunity to heat up with you but like always you be gone gone gone. Guess if I do my job and you do yours then everybody will be happy but if we both fail or one of the other then all fails right? I have another letter coming cause I got to get back to my job and do what all these brains want...communication. See you love.

Nefertum Husia Shayheh

Venus,

The one always having me caught up between delivering to others and loving myself. Like I never understood why we together by ourselves in a soul system but…you know what I don't even know what to say now. It is like we are there but not there. I try to put the intelligence into structure within a family model in today's time of you being at home on acres of land loving loving and loving all around right? You make the Empire so beautiful and too attractive. There is justice in you everywhere from the roses I think of all the time. For real, I do not want but I need love too; oh I cannot say that then I reveal my true self eh? The lover of all loves cause we share loves and I know all about your loving so to me I know when you come around. For reasoning known, our time apart allows me to pump up the volumes of intellectual inspiration with more energy to invest into business like providing my own culture see. See I know about love and beauty too of course. Being around you all the time loves become first nature though many of the times for myself. I try and am mastering myself, you know the mind, just in case if I happen to communicate with someone earthly, cause I do rule over earth below to be above, using your love to connect them in a high spiritual form where they never gone before is my duty. And you see, all those opportunities of bridging matters over I get to see what is what and who is who and where is which and how is why to find a love for me see. Knowing if I approach those loves you have for some other mission I know of cause after all I have to know cause I am the one communicating everything you know? It hurts the overall big picture of love; so I have a gift of loving myself and knowing two entities of gender plus much more to end up as this, well, angel? Or maybe just a shaman? Maybe a super-healer? Maybe a spiritual being disguised working on his and her mastery of the brain mastered by the divine mind sustaining to intensify my purpose on earth while actually being in another place at the same time? Indeed it is tragic when approaching beings cause they see love written all over me. They "feel" me and so therefore they are attracted in whatever loving way you have on them so I make sure I "analyze" them all, especially the female beings. It is like I am cursed with females cause by natural law we all know each other right? Though an aspect of me is just known straight out and I really do want that relationship of just communication between them all like roses in the wild or compacted in a bush or maybe creeping together through the nights just to arrive at somebody's doorstep in the day. We took our time crawling to grasp onto whatever handles of strength we could as one more notch of victory bringing sweetness and musk to mush them all into melts with their favorite smile eyes rolling back eyelids kissing eyelashes curling up of bliss. How sweet it is to deliver love and be so highly compassionate within those moments like a sexual act without physical intercourse. You feel as if your job is well done. I have come to the conclusion that I will never be able to love a female and have kids due to having the same loving ability as you mimicking the female exactly. Sometimes she just halts with mirror-like tendencies as if we were born to be forever and we are see cause love is like that to the endless. Though I am already married to love and she goes everywhere I go yet if I were to take one of those females again to a place of neverending like you Venus but on a higher trip into the spiritual super connection she will explode. Like you Venus, I have the power to be everywhere at once via tele-communication and deep emotional feelings as if our intuition were the seas, oceans, deltas, lakes, rivers, creeks, streams, into her like geyser purely rejuvenating to be wonderfully one of kind loved, yet I must do business plus relate messages as a sage to others. So emotions flare up between me and the female though I know I could never really harm such a lovely being but when she do not love me not knowing thyself then I have no other choice and must leave her as that final decision was made. Now I know Venus...what am I doing on earth anyway right? I get in trouble everytime so I stay to myself and try not to put out love or be myself but Venus we grew up together so there is no way to hide love, especially when you are a communicator as Oneness the soul cause I have found soul. Venus, I might say some harsh things about earth but it is because you got them wailing and over-zealous pumped up out of their humbleness with extravagance. So I cannot communicate with beings sometime when they are gone blown to the dome. Yet, I learn to listen more and more rather than forcing them to listen to me cause that is not communication of proper giving and receiving you see. I use my intellect while on earth in a quick, fast, concentrated plus focus to be concise precisely of all ways combined to apply a change invisibly while they are unconscious day and night. So I observe to find the right moments and angles when those are sleep cause playing with egos are like playing with suns at high noon—dangerous ain't that right rooster? So Venus I fight physical love every day and every night though I do enjoy looking into those eyes you tell them to seek out and find love of you, so I only glance once or twice and never too long cause I too will fall prey to your forces doing more damage on earth than providing solutions in the higher plane where I belong. I love you too but don't tell no-one. I like being the invisible man on earth but the invisible man will never be able to receive love...though knowing you will always be around allows me to give out more cause I know you give back making everybody and everything to an extent livable plus alright. I have to get back to work Venus like always cause you are slow as time can be made to be loved. Somebody right now is probably making slow love while I am writing this letter to you knowing when I lay my body to rest I have to work some more fleshless in a few hours. Sometimes I do think I am cursed with communication just as you with love but I do reap the benefits of being me minus the females now. It is more about peace within and enjoying some of my loves like roses, lotuses someday, oh and the butterfly gardens too, oh and the garden mazes and you know all my wishes going to come true cause I got my mind made up. I dare not wish you in the physical form any longer; I know better. Look for my letter always cause love is always on my mind now let me get back to business Venus.

Nefertum Husia Shayheh

Venus,

Another time of honesty with you I spend often giving away away a way of ways say down below bounces up and down. I stretch out feeling the below curved hugging me skin and why has below stiffen? I will never know why. If there were no numbers then size would not exist. Who cares about words of ecstasy and bliss while grinding me teeth hoping penetration could exist forever. See on earth love is define through each and every eyes from touches whom tongues lack certain knacks yearning two ears heard about those thoughts sift and smack and yes! I entered slowly as she said silently eyes closed he loves finally though her type of loving I will never know about as physical loving minus all others is a realm above us all yet around us all still below us center eye saw. See I do not possess the big bang yet measured and found myself often measuring bangs potential just to elude own self confidence. It is not my fault see as the world has compromise their own ability to be satisfied and go beyond the norm between two nope nowadays it is numerous. I have never done anything wrong to a female really Venus though being in the earthly storm between genders allowed me to see what is going on and how it have be going on since the beginning of my time though I try to get deeper to find out why of all their times without his stories and her stories just to find out indeed it is a super power trip of the sexes. Everytime I have felt you inside a female her heart whispered love me lover cause I know you do plus I will not fight you if you only just love me so deeply...and they say love conquers all so there you go Venus with war on your side. I will never know how deep is love and my soul cannot afford to go where love dwells unknown. I am my own being and chose to be wisest as in these days of times the womb has no heart though once upon ah time I could feel the beat of pulsation vibrating magick so splendid oh yes let me be the one to take her up up up as she takes me with her too up up up and away gasping for air of which life clings bottomless. So you learn to never play into the womb as I never did though only wanting me to produce truth of I as Me without drama yet scripts are played as love and beauty brings into character anew day. Why sexual attraction on this level? Well let us bring it back to the brain and mind getting Oneness Venus as this below bang will remain softer now as thoughts of physicality roams about of its own...and so I use the intensity to fuel my writing instead of getting excited to find someone to empty into my vain of pleasure and pain lasting only moments driving kisses upon tongues twisting hearts of lusty adventures where soft toes hold on to nothing but passionate breathing my oh my oh my loves from you Venus could possibly have sweats beading to perspire from within themselves as emotions are too much you see to be deeper into all the seas where secrets lie and truth seeks meek leak knots two hands hold onto ropes of neverending plots lots of fun for us tons of loves stuns evens oddly enough I love nibbling ear slightly telling her of us how our going is going two get sucked and such. She smiles with a blush and within me too I felt us raw and uncut swinging rhythms like never before ever

galore clever once forth back no more

made us soar tears we poured years of

happiness from our cores as oneness from

the brain and mind is how I figured inside

myself while walking two steps at ah time

outer as my inner-self to the depths on

earth I am creeping to come up as I have

already crept down to come back again as

the position from where you thought I had

left from within the darkness of the

spacious nights and our flight was

tremendously risen tendered letting go of

the string we float joyfully like kite. I cannot lie about loving love so I keep to myself wanting nothing but the pure finest dessert after each supper maybe by myself butt naked walking out the doors of my manse upon plush grasses picking a rose hearing wombs thunder and the rain falls down gently upon my skin yet it will not for a lifetime once my last breath is gone, so I rush back into my home all alone satisfied to be live smelling five below and five up high. I grow-up like rose beautified in my own way everlasting my own say today and tomorrow whether stiffen or soft together I release out of where no one has and will ever mark again...and that is my soul and heart. I cannot afford a female Venus as you have taught me the lessons so much beyond materials and her body is only an illusion which is a great memory of my greatest imagination and smile even harder once the moon's glow hasten. I will never truly know love inside and out and leave your power be giving you much credit due while we remain together in our system though orbiting on my own how. Why must love and beauty always brush against intelligence with spiritualness? Why can peace never be won? The effect of it will be too strong for anyone to ever hold-on. It is the truth especially in earth's society and when you dig deeper into the niches…it is very true within the original man and woman of where they are residing. Let me go again Venus as my journey must continue building up my own culture without a physical female to represent as symbolism cause I do admire business hoping one day to build an economy where few can eat free and many can be well. I just stretched out again the stress of me muscles out and now I must rumble in the jungles. Love you Venus.

Nefertum Husia Shayheh

Venus,

After traveling around the earth from land mass to land mass mixed in with quarrels to ideals of who am supposed to be versus who I am without flesh dictated by books on end of authors who wrote their version of life and yet science ends at the bone see. Love can you see all the color spectra? I bet you can and sow can I borrow your eyesight please? Can you lend yourself to the others who are blind eh? In every language there is a difference as a whole put together limited of what they know based on what they concluded together to be true. I am not philosophical nor am I the truth though I am a time traveler one who is the wind lofty and about certain ways and there you go again. I wonder, why I cannot be great? Well of course other intelligent forms use the england-ish oppression though who cares about their atmosphere eh? I feel really comfortable knowing who I am without types pinned down on me. Who wants to be a color? Who wants to be a nationality? They war constantly for the supreme of who is the best idiot on earth when others of other planets or so called stars named which name is a symbol itself vibrating into an existence called real once you are taught it is by the masters who is she and he at birth...I went boom just now. Better than my last times is what I pursue and to never come back on earth shackled like an infant knowing I am able to grow-up myself you see. I do not need no approval from anybody to be great in my own light as I came in alone and so therefore I am going out alone as well. I see why the gopher only comes up at a certain time. I see why the snake avoids all hue-mans at all cost. I see why the butterflies can never be truly captured together. I see why the ants keep marching on throughout the weathers. I see why lizards camouflage themselves sitting in peace. I see why the birds only sing notes and certain pitches. I need that type of air you see. Only notes between her and I but she will never listen so therefore never learn. Wisdom is great. Respect is to be earned. Love is yearned. Envy is measured. Lost is found. Good is bad. Dictionary is thesaurus. Out of their mindset into my own I as Me of my own economy which inhabits my own culture and business I make by myself see. When you have tried and the past have tried harder then why I am trying hardest going nowhere in the present with the future who is not moving forward? Yes it is insanity I tell you love. It is crazy indeed. I rely on the, well understood the ancient intelligence in my own light without even going to those walls in the physical that indeed intelligence with power across the brain mastered mind you can create your own to grow throughout space and time. Either you keep creating or stop it. Once I create my own then I am stopping...as simple as that. I must create my own love and beauty you see. I must create my own business and economy you see; day and night with the pen of less words spoken. My language will not be of spoken words as words spoken created sounds affecting perception of what could be peace now turned into war as mindsets of egos battle to understand difference of planes during elemental gatherings not knowing each and every thing is everything.

The All is the All. Industrial nation is a large tribal situation. A tribe is a compact better regulated family without need to dominate. Though both are connected needing one another since discovery of each other now those two entities like before keep the fight up, and battles within claps the enlightenment down so war is inevitable among us all as surface mountains to valley bodies of memoirs of greatness loved to each culture versus hatred of disgust in the mouths of each other. Love go to the east and see if they hate the west. Love go to the north and see if they despise the south. I have been there and done that and if I am going to fight for anybody, it will be for myself. Venus I have been in a uniformed military just as the civilians on ground got their own and see once you are equipped with books of this and that nobody knows who you are except what you represent while inside that uniform. Imagine being labeled a color inner-sight among the lands of the hearts and heartless will you love? Yes…it is on on-sight now depending on how your mindset is so it is getting even deeper but at the same time ridiculous to even sit up and laugh to a joke about yourself being a hypocrite when spirit, soul, emotion and mental plane cannot be seen though only when you create it to grow. It is the five senses and more below who war while the five senses and more above knows nothing of that such but peace. Ever wonder why the woods are so calm versus the cities? Now take the cities as rambling egos versus the woods are higher consciousness. The air is cleaner to include serenity is felt in the woods versus in the cities. I am a woodsman and cannot lie about it so I know I must go back to where it is most understanding for me. And when they come and ask me who am I, I will tell them who I am minus all cultures and nationalities as anew even without people on my land cause they can think how they want to think while I think how I need to think. Problem is solved. Solution is love from within yourself and of yourself as everybody and most people you know will not understand themselves at all. So why carry danger around with you? Why carry fear around with you? Let all of what you have known simple go...cause like you Venus if they are then they will come back but totally grown-up in higher consciousness. Luckily for me Venus my heart has stopped once...so I know the truth for myself and not of no others you see. I can only see what I see versus what they see and it is best to see what I see versus kept shackled of what they see constantly derailing me off path of my journey as all people cannot go with you on your journey;

only yourself. Thanks you for listening

Venus and love you too.

Nefertum Husia Shayheh

Venus,

I like apples Eve and Venus. I love all those fruits. Say how about those moments along the Potomac River when lovers take strolls, wings fly around themselves, leaves fall gently, grass is soft though crisp for knits and light finger food munchies gathering, and benches are cold while some remain warm for another soul. I use to walk to the boulders with my glasses young cut buffy not stocky nor thick of how they be saying body types these days, though indeed athletic statue of a guy pen in hand as well as my notebook. I always felt safe among strangers who was not paying attention steadily enjoying their lives as is, while I took advantage of peace of solitude sitting by the rocks at the bay. Everybody always was concerned of why he ain't doing like we do and all that stuff you know what I'm saying Venus? Yes, you remember as you had me writing my feelings to myself on those papers activating an invisible being up under the moonlight appealing to myself as everybody knew I was outer sight. Those days and nights feel so right still as if I am still reliving those moments warm and cut by those wind chills skin deep regardless of clothing layered. Like I never understood those reflections across waves of waters when nature visited hearing laughter in the background with feet patting breaths huffing and if you went silent into yourself you can even hear those tongues and lips slurping to kiss faces smacking. All in my mind though actually turning around to see them do this in action...I was dayum I want sum too!! But I learned quickly over the years that physical love is not for everybody and I tried the physical loving to the absolute everything almost and not so much as sexual but sentimental, compassionate, a massage, let me cook and bake, and I promise to rub your into a nice relaxing bath or wash you while we in the shower making purple rain yet nothing could make her be fulfilled that I was serious enough within the relationship to forward our reign. She never believed in us as royalty though only as her only. Maybe she was afraid I was just as beautiful as her equally and ready to be an aspirant pursuit of me and her full-time loving me always in your mind and heart until it stop pumping kind of loving. Yes indeed I have made females lovesick cause they did not expect me to give back love equally and more then more then some more and some more and you get the picture. I was real and still am nine hundred percent times my six names put together as three. Knowing what I know now along with wisdom allows me to see no-one is for me…why even front and fake? It takes a special soul for me to love and she don't switch up on me like I'm not there or something listening to her outer entities knowing good well her heart thumps more love and insight than any. I mean why not let her from within out the prison she is being held-in? Why not let her out cause after all when those females in the past use to be like saying "Why are you doing this to me? You know I love you? So what you mean?" Really that is their "inner royalty" speaking to them while directing miss communication at me see. The indirect games of leave her alone but you stalking me and stuff really feeling me to beyond means you cannot explain and so let the rationality leave your grasp to roll and rock with love like you be saying all the time to the world with that damsel in distress woe is me reflipped remixed rehunged redone rescrewed in some many emotional ways until it is quite pathetic from all ages pulling out all sorts of tricks that only Venus could do and uh oh...I said her name. Have you ever kissed lips why eyes were crying? It is like a ritual of tasting her sorrows and happiness drowning in her wettest sympathies knowing you have to heal her and the warrior of love comes out holding hands tightly squeezing palms feeling the heartbeats of the two of you from beginning to ending and she loves it cause love finally gets all the victory inside and out of how many ever times her soft toes and fingers and of course soft tip of her nose meets your to confirm you are one by her dominant indirect loves. Females be tripping me out Venus...you got them tripping on something else right about now but I keep coasting slapping high fives leaving them with funny faces like is he happy or playing with me or just him or why he did anyway? And you can feel they fingers slide down slow or clasped your whole hand and I be like whoa I done did it and showed myself you know the "love" and quickly tuck it back in as I have no clue of what is going on their lives. I'm a lover and not a fighter though I do box and I got skills in the stick-man arts really though! I love all females as they be truly trying to find love in all the wrong places on purpose too! Curious as a cat and when they find me they are like "wow we actually have so much in common" yes we do and maybe it is supposed to be like this as we are a part of the soul and spirit and not for your agenda of emotional attachment of a friend on keeps like standby as if I were a ball of yarn of fascination to be unravel with your kitty claws sharp and soft at the same depending on the strokes upon your back and belly is how I get pushed and pulled around kitty kitty kitty! No more meow around here cause it is all sssss King Cobra style and I don't mean in between your legs liquor phonetic type of sounds either, nope.

Cats are just as intelligent as snakes though I prefer to watch my own back gliding upright hood spanned sliding royal representing who I am secretly through the nights and enjoying the sun upon my rock during the great mourning hours in the day. Twenty-four seven my life is at stake cause I am just trying to love myself. Venus, loving is truly a test of times and being responsible for myself is enough loving besides taking on somebody else's love. I done tried that too with sensible solutions to carry-on past those problems and guess what? I could not solve them but at least she "heard" them though. And they gone keep saying there is no real men and etc. just as I am saying this of love from my experiences so a wall will continue to be constructed though not by me anymore but purely you Venus, goddess of love and war. I salute you just as you salute me. Peace and love while I dip out of the atmosphere of being called a "frienemy". I can't be called that when I am building up my own small economy non-illegal style and nobody is down cause unity in the all nationalities isn't happening while some stuck in fear and so much more so

guess what Venus? I'm in love by myself as

it is just me and you to the depths and

higher consciousness. One love and

Oneness.

Nefertum Husia Shayheh

QUOTES

40

"Love is everywhere like soul though without no name. I cannot have her all, yet in this lifetime we can enjoy sleepless nights together. My love."

"If i did not love you, then i would not be loyal. If i had no respect for you, then i would be dishonest. We share the same ideals."

"If my thoughts are free, then i feel freedom."

"Love is hatred from a different view. You do not want anybody to hold love except you."

"Where can I find love? Within myself."

"Love spoken entered inside spiraling around my ears. I felt her message ringing sensationally sincere."

"Who can I run into when my flesh needs love? My higher consciousness."

"I came across you before and so shall I again. Stay beautiful always my loves."

"She went from a knowledgeable seed who grew into wisdom. She stood strong as wisdom compassionately intelligent. She looked into the mirror to see Princess. Princess walked outside to be greeted as a Queen. Queen moved with power through prophecy and saw herself as an Empress. She told the world *checkmate*."

"She asked me yesterday am I married. She asked today the same. She asks tomorrow without delay. Love is within me fore keeps. I grew up as love inside so i never married nor need to be. Do you have love?"

"She is fine. Over there she is cute. Right here she is voluptuous. Left out she is ugly. She is horrible. She is nothing. Come here rose under my wing and let us fly above where love and beauty always smile."

"Soul friends share one thing in common—eternal love."

"I feel you love me. There is no other emotion truer than love. Let us stay soul friends forever."

"If agony were a secret would you tell about us soul friend? Remember our seal."

"When no bodies are around, two birds sing songs only kisses wish they felt. You feel our hearts beating now?"

"You never spoke love. We always series in our cove. Every time i want to go outside you finally say "NO!" Pulling me closer."

"Love has no eyes, yet my eyes can envision inside her all ways."

"She who loves hardest is really softest inside; ask tickle."

"Rings are for us love. Count how many wonderful years we have stood tall and strong alone in the wilderness of jealousy and envy. Each ring makes you smile proudly."

"We have our season when love is consciously intelligent and spiritual. Then love is fiery passionate and prophecy. Next love calms into a groove reflecting our deepest compassionate memoirs. Finally love analyzes our growth to create more fruitful tales of our soulful perfections. Exception is where love is without seasons, instead one of wholesome mystery."

"Love me knot. Love us roped. Love us undying hope."

"She found me telling my story. I wonder about her. I seen her face. I can write about her secretly without anybody knowing it is her."

"She will be my treasure and joy to write about forever. Finally, someone liked me enough to be lovingly true. I love her dearly."

"Embarrassment comes when you feel relieved. I felt relieved when understanding I love thyself."

"Why do I have to follow your loves, when I can create my own path?"

"Some people say love is a tradition. Many people say love is a religion. Several say love is a color. Most say love is a nationality. I only believe in myself so therefore rose is my faith."

"If you traced my bones back to the beginning of time, you will find an ending. How can I be periods and eras, when love is forever? Love was here before existence came into; though not of the word called love."

"I tried loving female personally. I will never try loving male personally. She and I have missed communication. He and I are mirrors so love is not sexual between me and him. Love thyself I as Me spiritually. I am all I focus into now."

"Religions could not satisfy me. There were chains still held in place over mind. Being a race could not exempt me from war. Being a color could not truly identify me into a nationality. Being a nationality could always expose me to a tribal battle. Being a gender separates me from the opposite. I came up with a plan...accept who i am to them while thinking and accepting who i am of within me; and stay outer sight."

"When you go against one notion, ultimately you go against the world as everything is tied in together. You are doomed unless your love keeps you warm at night and day."

"There is no unity when everybody wants a piece of love. There is only unity when resting in peace perceptively."

"Love sleeps while love is awake. Sun shines west and so does moon glow east. Stars are everywhere as galaxies are more than we think. Love is awake while love sleeps."

"I learned to never put love into a hue-man being hands. Hue-man beings never last."

"My culture is all about love of how soul views it. Therefore my business must be everywhere to grow a loving economy. Love is soul as spirit is known."

"Love is no-thing. Yet we place value on an object from our subjectivity to show and prove we indeed know, see, hear, taste and feel love."

"Fear is more powerful than love. Just ask Venus when she comes around."

"Have you read yourself lately? Where is your love?"

"When you can look back on the books you have written to smile…you know then you must have loved yourself cause after all, those are your words from within. Know thyself."

"Authors give a sharing point of view of their lives. I have read many authors from when I was in elementary school up until now. When am I going to share my point of view of my life?"

"As long as I have love then I know deep within my heart, I will always be great. Let me shine beautifully brighten without bad arrogance and bad ignorance."

www.ingramcontent.com/pod-product-compliance
Lightning Source LLC
Chambersburg PA
CBHW071811170526
45167CB00003B/1265